Connecting Worlds: The Coffee Trail

From farmer to consumer

Olaf Hammelburg

Connecting Worlds Productions

CONSUMER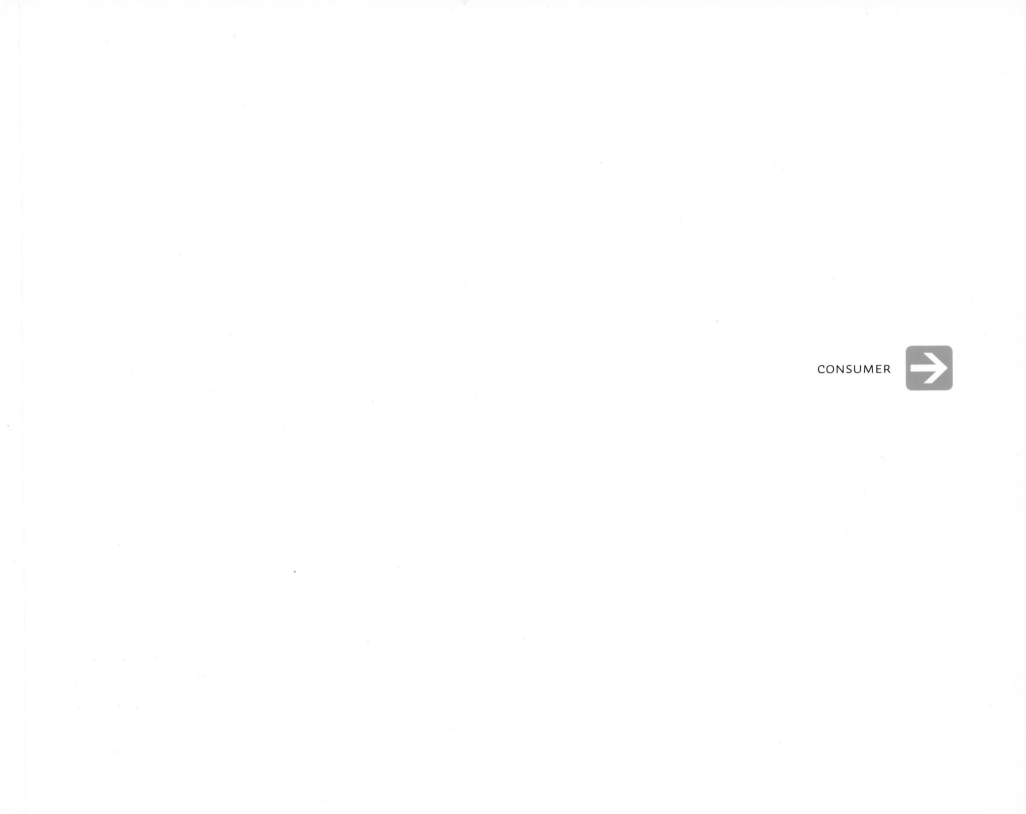

COFFEE BEANS ARE SEEDS. THEY ARE INSERTED INTO
THE SOIL AND THE BEAN IS PUSHED UPWARDS, BURSTS
OPEN AND THE LEAVES GROW OUT OF IT. HERE IS A
COFFEE PLANT DURING ITS FIRST FEW DAYS.

The photos in this book were taken in all the major coffee-production areas in Peru, South America. However, most of them show the route described on this map: a long difficult journey over muddy paths, rough rivers and high snow-covered mountains. The route winds through Peru's radically different climatic zones: the Selva (the Amazonian jungle), the Sierra (the Andes mountains) and the eternal mist of the Costa (the coast).

In the 1970s, people descended from the Sierra to the high slopes of the Amazon in search of work. They started to cultivate coffee, and thus was Putina Punco established. In Peru, coffee is produced solely by smallholder coffee farmers; that is, farmers with a small piece of land, on average 6 acres. Apart from Brazil, all countries in Central and South America mainly consist of small-holder coffee farmers. Although their yields are smaller, they are often capable of producing the finest flavors.

For this book, I picked just one route from one country. However, it serves as a symbol for every other route that coffee takes from small-holder farmers to the consumer.

In designing the book, we have included some extras which help you to read the book both ways: from farmer to consumer or vica versa. It's all about bridging the gap between these two worlds.

* Coffee production areas

OLAF HAMMELBURG (BORN 1970, BAARN, THE NETHERLANDS) GRADUATED IN ECONOMETRICS AT THE UNIVERSITY OF GRONINGEN IN 1995. AFTER WORKING AS A COMPUTER PROGRAMMER FOR A FEW YEARS, HE DECIDED TO DEDICATE HIS LIFE TO PHOTOGRAPHY AND FILMING. FOLLOWING A YEAR'S STUDY AT THE PHOTOACADEMY IN AMSTERDAM, HIS CAREER TOOK OFF - WITH ONE OF THE HIGHLIGHTS HERE IN YOUR HANDS.

WWW.OLAFHAMMELBURG.NL

CONNECTING WORLDS: THE COFFEE TRAIL, BY OLAF HAMMELBURG

'DO YOU SEE THE WORLD THAT LIES BEHIND YOUR PACKAGE OF COFFEE WHEN YOU PLACE IT INTO YOUR SHOPPING BASKET? DO YOU TASTE THE CHAIN OF WORKMANSHIP THAT STRETCHES ACROSS SEVERAL CONTINENTS WHEN YOU DRINK YOUR ESPRESSO? THIS BOOK IS THE PHOTOGRAPHIC TRAVEL LOG OF A JOURNEY BETWEEN TWO TOTALLY DIFFERENT WORLDS THAT ARE LINKED BY THE SAME PRODUCT.'

I was very fortunate during the last couple of years. I had the opportunity to live next to the source of my daily cup of coffee. The unlimited hospitality of the farmers made it possible for me to stay, for several months at a time, at the heart of Peruvian coffee production. These experiences with coffee farmers were an encounter with the growers of a product I had drank four times a day – without ever knowing anything about its origin. Now coffee has acquired a face for me. When you know the people, and the hardships they endure to grow their coffee plants, drinking coffee becomes a different experience. It is the farmer's efforts that you will discover in a good cup of coffee. You are able to taste his experience and skills as you can in a special glass of wine. It is a glimpse into a world far from your own. With this book, I have endeavored to bring both those worlds closer together.

One of the most memorable and impressive destinations was Putina Punco, a village deep in the Peruvian jungle close to the border with Bolivia. It was an experience composed purely of two things: nature and coffee. It's a place where beautiful parrots fly over your head, and colorful tucans sway on green branches. To get there involves a remarkable trip. After a twelve-hour journey from the snowy peaks of the Andes to the dense forest, the road changes into a narrow pathway that leads into the jungle. We could go no further by car. Along this path, I saw men with bales of coffee walking one by one into the village. The fortunate ones had donkeys to carry their load, while others carried their bales on their shoulders. I was going to live with a farmer for a few days, but my guide told me that the walking paths were too difficult because of the rain – and that the only way to continue was to make a raft to drift down part of the river. We spent the night in a hut somewhere in the jungle.

The next day, we reached the farm. The farmer was flattered by my effort to visit his family's house; they had never seen somebody from the west

before. They had prepared a great meal with guinea pig, which rather than being a common pet is a Peruvian delicacy. The home of a farmer is small and primitive. They are made of clay bricks, and the floor is just soil. There is no running water and electricity. My bed consisted of 2 planks, supported at either end by coffee bales.

Rising for sunrise at 6am, we walked for two hours to reach the coffee field or chacra. We picked beans, standing on steep slopes for the whole day. Then the fully loaded bags had to be carried back to the farm, where they were processed the next day. The whole experience was an eye-opener for me. Coffee farmers complete more than 80% of all the work required to create a cup of coffee: they should not, therefore, remain anonymous. These people deserve much more than what traditional trade models give them as compensation.

To improve the livelihood of a coffee farmer there are many simple things you can do. You can look for packages with labels like Fair Trade, Rainforest Alliance or UTZ Certified. Alternatively, specialty coffees offer a diverse and interesting way to buy ethically. In recent years the specialty coffee market has grown rapidly, driven by people willing to pay higher prices to the farmers for the highest quality beans, and with a focus on direct relationships with the place of origin.

There are many ways of trade and different labels, each has its own virtues and strengths. May this book inspire you to investigate these for yourself. As I was inspired by the many people I met along this coffee journey, I hope this book will encourage you to start a personal journey of your own: one of buying better and fairer coffee, and that you will inspire others in turn.

Wishing you a 'Buen Viaje'!

KENNETH DAVIDS HAS PUBLISHED THREE BOOKS ON COFFEE: 'COFFEE: A GUIDE TO BUYING, BREWING & ENJOYING', 'ESPRESSO: ULTIMATE COFFEE', AND 'HOME COFFEE ROASTING: ROMANCE & REVIVAL'. HE CO-PRODUCED, HOSTED, AND SCRIPTED "THE PASSIONATE HARVEST," AN AWARD-WINNING DOCUMENTARY FILM ON COFFEE PRODUCTION. HIS INFLUENTIAL COFFEE REVIEWS APPEAR REGULARLY IN THE PRIZE-WINNING WORLDWIDE WEB PUBLICATION COFFEEREVIEW.COM. HE WORKS AS A CONSULTANT TO PRODUCERS, ROASTERS AND RETAILERS IN NORTH AMERICA, LATIN AMERICA, AFRICA, THE MIDDLE EAST, INDIA AND JAPAN.

KENNETH DAVIDS: FROM LABORERS TO COLLEAGUES 'THE TRADITIONAL WAY TO LOOK AT COFFEE HAS ALWAYS BEEN: COFFEE AS COMMON MAN'S LUXURY, THE WINE OF THE PEOPLE, AN INEXPENSIVE ELIXIR OF DEMOCRACY. COFFEE HAS LONG BEEN ENSHRINED AS AN EVERYDAY, ALWAYS AFFORDABLE PLEASURE. BUT THERE ARE TWO REASONS TO CALL THIS ASSUMPTION INTO QUESTION.'

First, this one-time everyman's luxury is no longer luxurious – not by anyone's standards. The commonplace coffee of supermarket and convenience store has long degenerated from simple but satisfying pleasure to blandly bitter habit. Second, from its very beginning, this everyman's luxury came at the cost of another everyman's suffering. Coffee traditionally may have been a cheap luxury for city folk, but only because the rural poor kept it that way through their unsung drudgery and sacrifice.

This book is in part a singular and intimate record of that sacrifice. It demonstrates that coffee has always been the product of an extraordinarily complex series of procedures – procedures that demand unrelenting dedication from a global community of collaborators, most of whom remain faceless and impoverished. As we come to know the faces and stories behind the anonymous labor of coffee, our response can lead us in two directions: directions that may seem antithetical, but in my view are complimentary. One response is to express our human solidarity with the nameless faces behind the coffee through programs like Fair Trade, which offer us the opportunity to support farmers by paying a bit more for coffees that return sustainable prices to them in return for their dedication.

The other direction leads us towards a fascination with coffee itself: with the devotion, acts and accidents that produce a drink we once took for granted, but have come to cherish as a valuable and vulnerable pleasure, worthy of focus and appreciation. Whether we respond as activists, connoisseurs or both, our response usually begins with an encounter. It may be an encounter with a book that leads us to the pursuit of coffee, or an encounter with coffee that sends us in pursuit of a book.

The revelation that occurs at tasting events is always twofold: mind and senses, the disclosure of the amazing story behind the coffee and the shocking pleasure of the coffee itself when freed from commodity-driven mediocrity. It can be a rediscovery – of an aroma, a complexity that was lost and forgotten but has now been found again. Or it may be the realization that coffee is not something one needs to bury under frothed milk and syrup, nor distort and simplify by partly burning it in the roaster, but the seed of a fruit that, treated with care, offers a natural sweetness and a varied and lyric beauty.

With this shock of the senses comes the revelation of history and culture – the immense and complex journey documented in this book.

Ultimately, if we are to achieve a world in which coffee is no longer taken for granted and takes its rightful place as a beverage as worthy of respect as wine, and if the producers of fine coffee are to become as well respected (and as well compensated) as vintners, I believe we need both the passion for the beverage itself as expressed in connoisseurship and the passion for human solidarity as expressed in Fair Trade.

For me, the finest outcome would see the Fair Trade seal – or something like it – become as common and inevitable on coffee as the "Dolphin-Safe" seal is on canned tuna – a rule rather than exception, something that no coffee can afford to come to the market without. Simultaneously encouraging a sophisticated passion for the beverage itself would allow truly exceptional and distinctive coffees to attract prices that soar high above the Fair Trade minimum – and transform the creators of those coffees from faceless tropical laborers to familiar and celebrated colleagues.

WHEN THE SEEDLINGS ARE STRONG ENOUGH, THE FARMER PUTS THEM IN A DIVIDED BOX.

→ 10
← 103

→

ONCE THE COFFEE PLANT MATURES, THE FARMER BRINGS
THEM TO THE FIELD. USING A SOPHISTICATED METHOD,
HE CALCULATES THE DISTANCE BETWEEN EACH PLANT
AND AT WHICH ANGLE IT NEEDS TO BE PLACED. AFTER
BEING PLANTED IT CAN TAKE UP TO 4 YEARS FOR
THE PLANTS TO PRODUCE THEIR FIRST CHERRIES.
IN MOST REGIONS IN PERU COFFEE GROWS ON VERY
STEEP SLOPES. THE FARMER MAINTAINS HIS FIELD BY
CUTTING THE LOWER GROWING PLANTS AND LEAVING
THE LARGER TREES STANDING. THIS PROVIDES A SHADED
AREA WHICH PRODUCES A HIGHER QUALITY COFFEE.

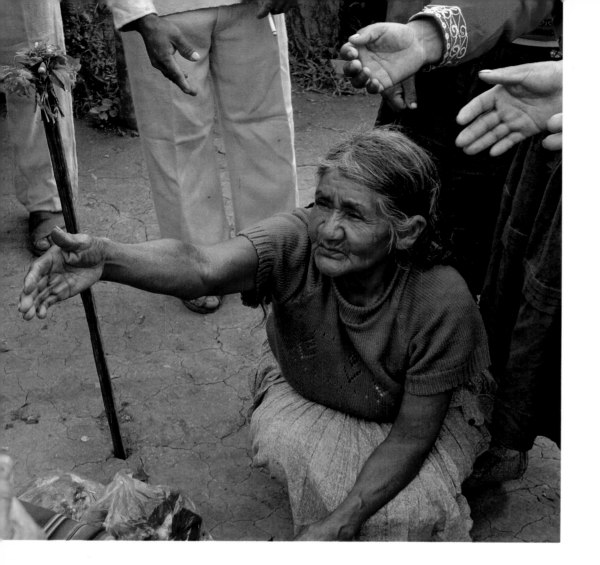

← →

IN THE REGION AROUND PUTINA PUNCO SOME FARMERS
STILL MAINTAIN OLD INCA RITUALS. THESE ARE PER-
FORMED BEFORE EACH HARVEST PERIOD. DURING THE
RITUALS, THE FARMERS SHAKE HANDS TO SHOW THEIR
COMPANIONSHIP AND TO PROMISE TO WORK TOGETHER.
THEN A SHELL IS PASSED AROUND, FROM WHICH THEY
DRINK WINE.

next two pages
DURING THE PRAYERS THEY PREPARE OFFERINGS FOR THE
GODS. THE OFFERINGS ARE A MIX OF COCA LEAVES, WINE
AND FLOWERS.

→

OFFERINGS ARE SPREAD OVER THE COFFEE-TREES BY THE SHAMAN, A HOLY MAN WHO LEADS THE RITUALS. IN THIS MANNER THE FARMERS PRAY TO THE GODS FOR A GOOD HARVEST.

next two pages
AFTER THE SHAMAN HAS MADE THE FIRST OFFERINGS, EACH MEMBER OF THE GROUP WILL PERFORM THEIR OWN INDIVIDUAL OFFERING. THE WOMAN WITH THE YELLOW SWEATER IS SPRAYING WINE OVER THE TREE WITH A FLOWER.

BEFORE STARTING THE HARVEST, SOME WORKERS SMOKE CIGARETTES, SINCE THE SMOKE GETS RID OF THE INSECTS.

← →

IN PERU ALL FARMERS PICK THEIR CROPS BY HAND.
HARVEST TIME LASTS AROUND 3 MONTHS BETWEEN
MAY AND SEPTEMBER; THE EXACT PERIOD DEPENDS
ON THE ALTITUDE. THE LOWER FIELDS ARE HARVESTED
EARLIER, WHILE THE HIGHER FIELDS ARE HARVESTED
TOWARDS THE END OF SEPTEMBER. HIGHER FIELDS
WILL PRODUCE BIGGER BEANS OF HIGHER QUALITY.
COFFEE BEANS GROW IN CHERRIES, WHICH WHEN
RIPE HAVE A RED OR YELLOW COLOR, DEPENDING ON
THE VARIETY. HOWEVER, NOT ALL CHERRIES RIPEN
SIMULTANEOUSLY, AND A SINGLE BRANCH CAN HAVE
BOTH RIPE CHERRIES AND UNRIPE CHERRIES.
TO REACH A HIGH QUALITY THE FARMER HAS TO PICK
ONLY THE RED OR YELLOW ONES AND LEAVE THE
GREEN ONES TO RIPEN.
THIS MEANS HE MAY HAVE TO VISIT THE SAME PLANT
UP TO 3 TIMES DURING THE HARVEST.

next two pages
DURING THE HARVEST PERIOD FAMILIES WORK
TOGETHER. THIS IS DONE ACCORDING TO AN OLD
INCA PRINCIPLE, AYNI. THIS PRINCIPLE STATES
"YOU DON'T GIVE WITHOUT RECEIVING SOMETHING
IN RETURN, AND YOU DON'T RECEIVE WITHOUT
GIVING SOMETHING IN RETURN".

→
A HANDFUL OF FRESHLY PICKED RIPE
COFFEE CHERRIES.

SERGIO MUÑOZ MAYO: LIFE HAS IMPROVED 'MUCH HAS CHANGED IN THIS AREA SINCE WE ORGANIZED OURSELVES INTO A COOPERATIVE. IN THE PAST, KNOWLEDGE WAS PASSED DOWN FROM GENERATION TO GENERATION. THERE WAS SOME IMPROVEMENT, BUT SINCE WE HAVE GAINED THE SUPPORT OF PEOPLE WITH A TECHNICAL EDUCATION IN AGRICULTURE, THE FARMING TECHNIQUES HAVE IMPROVED SIGNIFICANTLY.'

'Everyone in this area is a coffee producer. Entire families are involved with the harvest and the upkeep of the plantation. We wake up with coffee and dream about it at night. I first started as an independent coffee producer, but for the last seven years, I have worked in an organized fashion within a cooperative. Since we organized ourselves, much has changed. The selecting of the seeds, and the germinating and growing of the plants used to be done in a traditional way. In those days, sowing and harvesting was done without fertilizing and trimming the coffee bush. If we wanted to grow a coffee tree, we would just peel the seeds, dig a hole, and wait until a plant popped up.

'In the cooperative we have learned to apply certain agricultural techniques. A team of agricultural experts has shown us what fertile soil is, how to select seeds, how to take care of a seedbed, and how to make good compost out of natural raw materials without using chemicals. As organized producers, we are better able to reach the export markets. In the past, this was something reserved only for large companies and not for the small farmer. As a consequence, life has improved – not just for men but also for the women. They are now allowed to participate in the cooperative, even in management, and therefore have more access to knowledge. They are also allowed to benefit from the workshops and training. In this way, they learn everything about the market and the business.

'The improvements that we are now able to make are, in part, the result of increased awareness of our situation in the west. Fair Trade was the first to ensure that we were guaranteed a minimum wage. As small-scale farmers, we had always been a plaything of the large producers in countries like Brazil.

If Brazil would produce a surplus, the global market price would drop – and, by extension, so would our income. Fair Trade fixes a minimum price, which means that in such cases we are still guaranteed a minimum wage, regardless of the global coffee situation.

'Many more initiatives which aim to improve our lives have appeared in the market. But in order for them to work, the consumer does need to choose the right products. I have five children, and I believe that they deserve the chance to get a good education and personal development. Support from the cooperative and extra money from the Fair Trade market have allowed us to afford better teachers and teaching materials for the schools. We hope to soon also get a library and a hospital in our district.

'Unfortunately, we can only harvest once a year. The harvest time lasts two to three months. I myself have two hectares of land on which to grow coffee. On average, I produce 1,600 kilos of coffee beans per year; it depends on whether enough rain falls and whether or not the crops are struck by diseases. My dream is to start producing much more, to do more business and in this way be able to invest more in our plantation. But what is most important of all is that my children find good jobs, so that they can lead a better life than me. I don't mind if they work in coffee, but first they should study – they are, after all, the future of Peru. It would be great if one of my children would want to become an agricultural expert.'

SERGIO MUÑOZ MAYO (RIGHT) WORKING ON HIS FIELD. HE AND HIS WIFE ARE PUTTING THE FRESHLY PICKED CHERRIES INTO LARGE PLASTIC BAGS WHICH WILL BE BROUGHT TO THE FARM.

AFTER HARVESTING, THE CHERRIES MUST BE CARRIED
BACK TO THE FARM. HERE, A FAMILY USES A METHOD
WITH A BAMBOO STICK.

next two pages
SOME USE A MULE, OTHERS JUST A PLASTIC BASKET.
THE LADY WEARS TRADITIONAL PERUVIAN CLOTHING
FROM THE NORTH.

29 →
84 ←

FARMERS RETURNING TO THEIR FARM, WHERE THE
CHERRIES ARE COLLECTED FOR FURTHER PROCESSING.

BACK AT THE FARM THE CHERRIES ARE PUT IN A TANK
TO BE WASHED. THE SMALLER AND LIGHTER CHERRIES
WILL FLOAT AND BE SEPARATED; THEIR QUALITY IS
NOT HIGH ENOUGH FOR EXPORTING.

BENITA FACUNDO QUEVEDO: MS. PRESIDENT 'MY ELDERLY 86-YEAR-OLD MOTHER LIVED IN VERY DIFFERENT TIMES TO ME. SHE USED TO WALK WITH HER DONKEY THROUGH THE LOCAL VILLAGES TRADING HER COFFEE FOR OTHER PRODUCTS. TODAY, THANKS TO THE CEPICAFE COOPERATIVE, I AM ABLE TO EXPORT MY COFFEE ALL OVER THE WORLD. I ALSO HAD THE OPPORTUNITY TO BECOME PRESIDENT OF OUR LOCAL ASSOCIATION. WOMEN TODAY ARE GENERALLY TAKEN MUCH MORE SERIOUSLY. THERE IS, HOWEVER, STILL A LONG WAY TO GO TO BRING OUR STANDARD OF LIVING UP TO AN ACCEPTABLE LEVEL.'

'When I was younger, I did not enjoy working on the land at all. I preferred to trade groceries. But because my mother developed rheumatism, I was forced to become more involved in the cultivation of our coffee. This opened up a whole new world for me, which I became increasingly enthusiastic about. I began to discover the importance of being able to work your land well, to be able to grow your coffee in harmony with nature.

'This is reflected in particular in the principle of Pachamama, which originates from Inca times. Pachamama was thought to be a goddess of fertility, who watched over the crops. Her name is often translated literally as 'mother earth'. When we make a toast, we pour a little out of our glasses onto the ground and say 'Pachamama' – meaning 'for mother earth'. This follows the principle that when you take something from the earth, you also have to put something back. I try to apply this principle in the cultivation of my crops. In addition to coffee, I also have my own vegetable garden.

'Since I have taken the baton from my mother, many things have changed in our region. The coffee trade has always been a man's world. But when we decided to form cooperatives, we women gained more power in many areas. Not only in the local authority, but also in our dealings with clients. We became stronger. 'I have been the president of our organization, La Esperanza – which means "hope" – since 2002. This organization forms part of the umbrella cooperative Cepicafe. As an organization we have the task of ensuring that we cooperate well in times of harvest, that our finances are in good order and that the quality of our beans remains up to standard.

'In the past, it was quite common for any extra money that was earned to be immediately drunk away in the local café. Now we advise people on how to control their finances. With the extra money we hope to be able to buy a plot of land for the construction of a building where our meetings can be held. In addition, I am striving to get more women onto the committee and to get involved in trade work so that we spread our work a little.

'We still have a long way to go before we will permanently be able to live above the poverty line. Life is sometimes hard. We often only just earn enough to cover our day-to-day costs of living. There is not much left over to invest in a better future. We are still dependent on initiatives from the west to improve trade. Fortunately, more and more of these initiatives are being introduced and our hopes for the future remain vested in them.

For this reason I will do everything in my power to make La Esperanza even stronger.'

BENITA TAKES OUT THE FLOATING CHERRIES, WHICH WILL BE USED FOR LOCAL CONSUMPTION.

→

AFTER THE BERRIES HAVE BEEN WASHED THEY ARE PUT IN THE *DESPULPADOR*, A MACHINE THAT REMOVES THE SKIN OF THE BERRIES. REMAINING ARE THE SO-CALLED *PERGAMINO* BEANS. THIS IS THE THIN-SKINNED GREEN BEAN, WHICH WILL EVENTUALLY BE ROASTED.

next four pages
MOST FARMERS OPERATE THE MACHINE BY HAND, ALTHOUGH SOME HAVE INVENTED A MECHANIZED PROCESS USING A BICYCLE.

THE BEANS ARE PUT IN A FERMENTATION TANK, WHERE THEY FERMENT FOR AROUND TWO DAYS. DURING THE FERMENTATION, TWO MAIN PROCESSES TAKE PLACE: BACTERIA EAT THE SWEET LAYER AROUND THE BEAN, AND THE SWEET LAYER IS CONVERTED TO ALCOHOL. FERMENTATION IS A VERY IMPORTANT STEP IN MAKING A HIGH QUALITY COFFEE. CALCULATING THE DURATION OF FERMENTATION IS DIFFICULT AND DEPENDS ON VARIABLES SUCH AS ALTITUDE, CLIMATE, AND VARIETY OF THE BEAN.

AFTER FERMENTATION THE BEANS ARE WASHED IN SMALL CANALS. HERE, A SELECTION PROCESS TAKES PLACE. THE HEAVIER, HIGHER QUALITY BEANS WILL STAY IN THE FIRST CANAL, WHILE THE LIGHTER ONES WILL FLOAT INTO THE NEXT CANAL.

WHEN WASHING IS COMPLETE, THE BEANS ARE LAID OUT TO DRY IN THE SUN.

A FARMER SHOWS A PERGAMINO BEAN. THE SKIN WILL
BE REMOVED WHEN THE BEANS ARRIVE IN LIMA.

next four pages
THE PERGAMINO BEANS ARE LEFT TO DRY IN THE SUN
FOR AROUND 3 OR 4 DAYS, DEPENDING ON CLIMATE
AND ALTITUDE. AFTER EACH DAY THE BEANS ARE PUT
BACK IN RACKS, FOR STORAGE DURING THE COLD
NIGHTS. THE NEXT DAY THEY ARE PUT IN THE SUN
AGAIN. DRYING IS A DELICATE STEP IN
PRODUCING HIGH QUALITY COFFEE. THE BEANS
ARE VERY SENSITIVE TO ODOURS AND IF STORED OR
TRANSPORTED WHEN TOO WET, THEIR QUALITY COULD
BE DIMINISHED.

EVERYWHERE IN AND AROUND PUTINA PUNCO, YOU
WILL FIND PEOPLE BUSY WITH COFFEE. IN THEIR
HOUSES THEY SORT THROUGH PILES OF DRIED BEANS,
PICKING OUT THE BAD ONES.

THE WHOLE FAMILY WILL BE HELPING SORTING THE
BEANS. HERE YOU SEE THREE GENERATIONS:
GRANDMOTHER, AND HER DAUGHTER BREASTFEEDING
THE (GRAND)DAUGHTER.

RAÚL SUPO MAMANI: ORGANIC FARMING. 'CULTIVATING USING ORGANIC METHODS MEANS NO LONGER GOING TO BED WITH A HEADACHE – AND EVERYTHING GROWING ON MY PLANTATION NOW LEADS A HEALTHIER LIFE.'

'The coffee growing region around Putina Punco is still relatively new – the first inhabitants came here around 1970. My own family moved from the upland plains surrounding Juliaca to the high hills of the jungle. Because there was no work we began to grow coffee here.

'I myself have lived in the area around Putina Punco since 1985. I took over the coffee plantation from my father. Back then, many chemicals were still used to combat certain diseases. We actually had no idea what we were doing. The chemical dealers had a lot of power, and they often sold us their products with nonsense stories; they didn't even know what was in it

'In 2003, I received a certificate which proves that I am a organic farmer. This means that I now only use organic methods to maintain my land. I not only take care of our land, but I also protect our surrounding environment. This took a lot of energy and time to achieve. Chemicals were easy to use – just spray a little here and there, and you would be finished. Now we have to search for 'a natural solution' in the form of traps for the pests. Thankfully, we receive a lot of support from the CECOVASA cooperative. They have people working for them who have studied for this.

'Many Quechua Indians live in this area, and when working we employ the principle of Ayni. This is the Inca concept of reciprocity: in general terms it means you don't give without receiving something in return, and you don't receive without giving something in return. In our case, this sees us gather as a group to help a particular family. This family will then later work with the group to help yet another family. During the harvest period, once a week, we transport the harvest in bags to the acopio, the assembly point of our cooperative.

'For the farmers from my area, it is practical to transport the coffee using rafts. We make these every week from the inner tubes of trucks, rope, and wood from the forest. This method means that we run a greater risk of damaging the product; our community is in need of an improved infrastructure. At the acopio, our coffee is inspected. Engineers from CECOVASA inspect the coffee by means of spot checks. They measure the moisture level, the average size of the beans, and the percentage of bad beans. If the coffee gets the green light, we are paid.

'In 2007 we got paid US$140,50 per 46 kilogram bag. The cost of production for one bag is around US$98. I produce 20 bags a year, so I gained US$850. Before then, we weren't used to making that much – we had years where the sales price was more or less equal to the cost price, so back then we were not making any money.

'I hope that my children will be able to study, so that they can then work as agricultural advisors. However, there isn't enough money for that yet. Profits in 2007 were just enough to be able to support my family, but there is no money for a good education, clean water or electricity. I would also very much like to travel more to other countries, to learn about other cultures, but the most important thing to me is that my sons be able to study, so that they won't be forced to stay here and work on the plantation like me.

'It is not only the business world that should take responsibility. Local and national governments in my country should work towards building a better future. For that reason, it is important that we stay organized and work together.'

RAÚL SUPO MAMANI (AT THE FRONT RIGHT) TRANSPORTS HIS COFFEE IN WELL-SEALED BAGS ON A SELF-CONSTRUCTED RAFT. DUE TO RAIN IT IS SOMETIMES IMPOSSIBLE TO TAKE THE PATHWAYS. BUILDING A RAFT AND GOING DOWNRIVER IS THE ONLY WAY TO GET HIS COFFEE TO THE COOPERATIVE ON TIME. THIS RISKY OPERATION WILL TAKE HIM UP TO 8 HOURS.

WHEN THE BEANS ARE PROPERLY DRIED AND
SELECTED, THEY ARE TRANSPORTED. AS EARLY AS 4
A.M., FARMERS LOAD THEIR MULES AND BEGIN THEIR
LONG TREK. DURING THE WALK OTHER FARMERS JOIN;
AT AROUND MID-DAY THEY ARRIVE AT THE *ACOPIO*.
AN *ACOPIO* IS A PLACE WHERE THE COOPERATIVE
HAS A SMALL, BASIC OFFICE, WHERE THE BEANS ARE
COLLECTED.

next four pages
NOT EVERYBODY HAS A MULE, AND SOME FARMERS
HAVE TO CARRY THE BAGS ON THEIR SHOULDERS.
TRANSPORTATION IS VERY HARD IN THESE REGIONS.
IT OFTEN RAINS IN THE JUNGLE, WHICH MAKES THE
PATHS SLIPPERY AND DIFFICULT TO TAKE; IN ADDI-
TION, PATHS ARE OFTEN SMALL AND NEXT TO DEEP
RAVINES. SOME FARMERS HAVE TO WALK FOR TWO
DAYS TO REACH THEIR NEAREST *ACOPIO*

54

59

→

AFTER ARRIVING WITH THE RAFT THE BAGS ARE UN-
LOADED AND BROUGHT TO THE ACOPIO

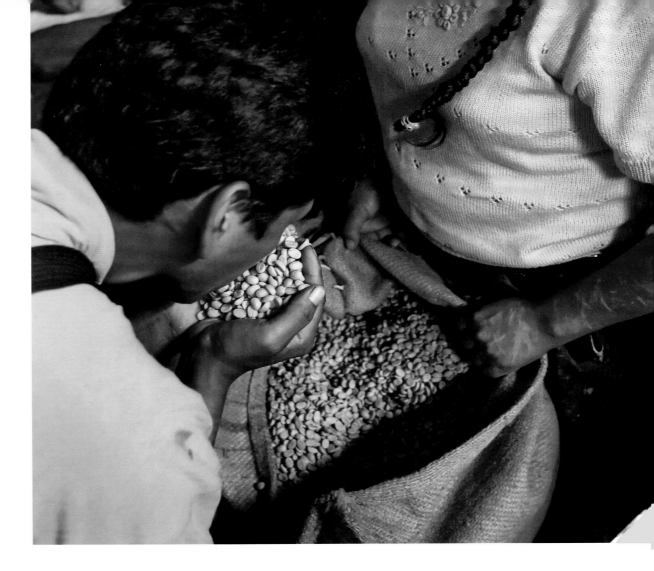

AT THE ACOPIO, TECHNICIANS CHECK THE BEANS
BY SMELLING THEM: IF THE BEANS HAVE NOT BEEN
STORED WELL THEN THEY MAY HAVE ABSORBED
TRACES OF SOIL, PAINT, GASOLINE OR OTHER
SUBSTANCES. SOMETIMES THEY CRACK THE BEANS
BETWEEN THEIR TEETH TO TEST THE HUMIDITY.

THE TECHNICIANS ALSO TAKE SAMPLES AND COUNT
THE NUMBER OF DEFECTS. DEFECTS ARE BEANS THAT
ARE CONSIDERED TO BE DAMAGED. TO BE SUITABLE
FOR EXPORT, THE BAGS MAY NOT CONTAIN TOO MANY
DEFECTS. INTERNATIONALLY THERE ARE SEVERAL
QUALITY STANDARDS THAT DEFINE THE NUMBER OF
DEFECTS PER KILO. IF THERE ARE TOO MANY DEFECTS,
THE FARMER MUST GO THROUGH HIS WHOLE BAG
AGAIN TO PICK OUT THE DEFECTS.

next four pages
WHEN EVERYTHING IS CORRECT,
THE BAGS ARE WEIGHED.

TO VERIFY THAT EVERYTHING IS HANDED OVER
CORRECTLY, THE FARMER MUST SIGN THE PAPERS.

AS MANY FARMERS ARE UNABLE TO READ OR WRITE,
SIGNING WITH A FINGERPRINT IS COMMON.

ONCE ALL THE PAPERWORK IS DONE,
THE FARMER IS PAID.

GEORGE HOWELL FOUNDED THE QUALITY-PIONEERING 'THE COFFEE CONNECTION', INC., IN BOSTON, IN 1974. HE RECEIVED THE SPECIALTY COFFEE ASSOCIATION OF AMERICA LIFETIME ACHIEVEMENT AWARD IN 1996. GEORGE CO-FOUNDED THE PRESTIGIOUS CUP OF EXCELLENCE™ IN 1999, A NON-PROFIT ORGANIZATION TO DEVELOP QUALITY FOR ROASTERS, PRICE BENCHMARKS FOR FARMERS AND A NEW GLOBAL COFFEE COMMUNITY NETWORK. IN 2007 HE WAS AWARDED THE SPECIALTY COFFEE ASSOCIATION OF EUROPE'S HIGHEST HONOR, THE BETTER COFFEE WORLD AWARD.

THE WINE OF THE TROPICS, BY GEORGE HOWELL IN AUGUST 2001, I DRANK AN EXCEPTIONAL CUP OF COFFEE OFFERED TO ME BY A SMALL PERUVIAN COFFEE GROWER. IT WAS REMARKABLY BETTER THAN MOST COFFEE BEVERAGES I HAVE HAD SERVED TO ME ON A FARM. THE GROWER'S SECRET? "I DRINK ONLY MY BEST COFFEE," HE SAID WITH PRIDE.

What a welcome surprise! I have been to some famous coffee farms and been offered instant coffee! Many coffee farmers don't drink coffee, let alone their own, and far more drink their worst, preserving the best for export. Unlike wine growers, coffee farmers, with a few notable exceptions, treat their product as a mere raw commodity. They do not fundamentally know what they make. The coffee-producing countries in which they live reflect the same attitude. Visit their beautiful lands, go to their best hotels and restaurants, where you can order the finest Bordeaux, and realize the coffee you are served is "consumo", low grade coffee, or not even from the country at all!

Sadly, the production of this small Peruvian coffee grower who loved his coffee was blended away with other small farmer lots of varying quality to produce the minimum commodity unit of 250 bags, nearly twenty tons of coffee. The wine of the tropics is still, for the most part, only a commodity. The best coffees in such a system can only achieve a better fair-average quality, good for latte drinks, nothing more—certainly nothing to rave about. Coffee-producing countries need to celebrate and fully differentiate the beverage their economies often depend on. Tourists should experience identified coffees that amaze them with their sweetness and the special flavors that only their terroirs can produce. Peru is such a country.....

In the summer of 2001, I cupped hundreds of small farmer lots to assess the potential of coffee quality produced by small farmers and cooperatives in Peru. One lot of 18 bags, less than 3,000 lbs., produced by a very small association of small growers, has become legendary in my memory. Here was a coffee of honeyed sweetness with clean fruit flavors unlike any other I have tasted. It was easy to pick out blind from all the others. If coffee aficionados could taste this coffee, what would they pay the

farmers? I called my sources in Peru, only to find out that it had been blended into a 20-ton lot, into anonymity. I have one 100-gram green sample of this coffee left, just enough for one roast. There it sits, vacuum packed and frozen. For me it is just like the last bottle of some great estate wine from a perfect vintage....
Drinking it will be a festive yet sad good-bye.

Few consumers realize what effort must go into producing fine, or even just fair average, quality coffee. It is a complex, time-consuming, difficult craft, rivaling in every way the challenges to produce fine wines. Ripe coffee takes nine months to develop from flower to ripeness, approximately double that of grapes, this in the tropics where a lot can go wrong. The harvest is next, when only ripe cherries must be picked, leaving unripes for another round. This may require up to five or even six separate passes. Next, the two beans, really seeds, must be extracted from the fruit without harming them. This involves depulping the outer skin of the fruit, then placing the mucilage-coated seeds in tanks, or basinets, where fermentation is allowed to take place until—and just until—the remaining fruit can be washed away with turbulent water, a process called washing. Many easy but costly quality mistakes can be made along the way, adding unpleasant flavors to the beverage. Drying the beans is the next very delicate task, when bean moisture must be driven down to just 10% to 12% for the beans to be stable. In the case of Peru this must often be done in cloud-shrouded mountains, where the best coffees grow. These are just the barest details. Add to all this the lack of infrastructure and resources in most coffee-producing countries and one begins to realize what a Herculean task the producer (grower-processor) has.

Coffee farmers have faced long years of hardship, during which coffee prices were below the cost of production, many losing their land and

others now so in debt that they simply subsist in the current market of prices hovering above basic costs. Many of the immigrants coming to the United States come from coffee farms fallen on hard times. They cannot compete against increasingly automated technified farms on flat lands producing for the mass market. The vast majority of the world's coffee farmers are on mountainsides, where almost all of the greatest coffees grow, requiring huge labor input. Such is the case with Peru. Small plot Burgundy-like quality-producing areas can be developed, giving these extraordinarily hard-working farmers a future free of charity dependence. Just as coffee-producing countries need to push for this to happen by creating real coffee cultures in their own backyards, as Brazil has been doing, coffee aficionados in the developed, consuming world need to pull.

Consumers have reacted very positively to the pioneering efforts of Fair Trade to raise awareness and improve the lot of small farmers, and rightfully so. Fair Trade has improved the lives of many and is part of the bouquet of valid approaches tackling farmers' welfare. But it is not enough; no single program can be. Fair Trade covers only cooperatives, does not address the needs of myriads of independent farmers (many of them owning less than 5 acres), has a long waiting list, and does not as yet address the possibility of farmers graduating out of the Fair Trade cocoon, which is fundamentally a voluntary payment system whereby the farmers are dependent upon the efficacy of their advocates and the good will of coffee businesses and consumers. How about independence as in the wine industry? Current Fair Trade prices paid by coffee roasters should be the minimum price paid for decent coffee, let alone fine coffee. We should demand and explore single origin coffees from identified, inspired farmers or small farmer groups that we can then reward with our pocketbooks and our repeat business. We live in an age of brands, of identity—and quality coffee farmers deserve no less. Fine coffees should

be sold by farm name (or smallest producing unit), region, variety, and then country, as with wine and fine teas. This would be a good start to blasting a hole through the commodity ceiling of farmer facelessness and would give those farmers with vision and commitment real rewards and opportunity. Coffee farmers ultimately need a platform where they can speak directly for themselves to us.

So let us consumers continue learning to savor our coffees more. Fine (non-espresso) coffee drinking is a sensual experience over time. It begins when the coffee is hot, when we can appreciate its complex floral, spicy, herbal, chocolate, sweet tobacco, and/or fruit-laden delicate aromas wafting from the cup, hinting of what is to come. When we have our first sip of hot coffee, only a small percentage of our taste buds are in action. It is still too hot. The flavor should be teasingly delicate, some-what hidden. Fine coffee should be explored as it cools and slowly reveals itself like a blossoming flower. The cooler the coffee gets, the more its character becomes pronounced, revealing layers of flavors and taste. Liveliness and body become fully perceived and appreciated with cooling. The aftertaste of a fine coffee should slowly and sweetly disappear. A truly fine coffee remains fully, wonderfully pleasant at stone-cold temperature, while others, less perfect, have lost their clean flavors and become grungy or insipid. The world of truly fine coffees has barely been scratched! What will you be drinking today? Cheers!

←

THE BAGS ARE LOADED ONE BY ONE
INTO A SMALL TRUCK.

next eight pages
ONE BAG WEIGHS AROUND 60 KILOS. THESE MEN ARE
LOADING BAGS THE WHOLE DAY, OFTEN BAREFOOTED
WALKING OVER SMALL PLANKS
IN AND OUT OF TRUCKS.

A MANAGER AT THE ACOPIO GIVES INSTRUCTIONS TO
THE MEN WHO ARE LOADING THE TRUCK. THE
COOPERATIVE HAS TO MANAGE EVERYTHING IN
DETAIL: WHICH BAGS BELONG TO WHICH FARMER,
THE BUYER OF EACH BAG, WHEN THE BAGS MUST BE
SHIPPED, AND MANY OTHER DETAILS.

THE LONG JOURNEY TO LIMA BEGINS. IT WILL PASS
THROUGH ALL THREE CLIMATE ZONES OF PERU,
BEGINNING WITH THE SELVA (WET RAINFOREST),
DOTTED WITH TINY VILLAGES.

THE ROUTE THEN CLIMBS INTO THE SIERRA, THE HIGH
MOUNTAINS OF THE ANDES, PASSING ROUGH RIVERS
ALONG THE WAY.

THE ROAD ALSO SNAKES THROUGH OLD INCA RUINS.
THE INCAS HAD A SOPHISTICATED SYSTEM OF
AGRICULTURAL PRODUCTION: HERE THE TRUCK PASSES
IMMENSE TERRACES WHERE THE INCAS ONCE
CULTIVATED THEIR CROPS.

THE PEOPLE OF THE HIGHLANDS ARE PERFECTLY
ADAPTED TO LIVE AT HIGH ALTITUDES. THIS BOY
PLAYING WITH A KITE HAS TYPICAL RED CHEEKS,
INDICATING THAT HE HAS MORE RED CELLS IN HIS
BLOOD – A TRAIT WHICH MAKES IT EASIER TO LIVE IN
THE MOUNTAINS.

WILD LLAMAS ARE SEEN ALONG THE ROAD
THROUGHOUT THE ANDES.

PASSING THE SNOWY PEAKS OF THE HIGHLANDS.
PEAKS IN THE ANDES CAN REACH ALTITUDES OF
AROUND 6,500 METERS.

← →

AFTER TWO DAYS THE TRUCK ARRIVES IN JULIACA, 4500 METERS ABOVE SEA LEVEL. HERE THE BAGS ARE LOADED INTO A BIGGER TRUCK, WHICH CONTINUES THE JOURNEY TO LIMA, THE CAPITAL OF PERU. THE TRIP FROM JULIACA TO LIMA TAKES TWO DAYS, WITH THE DRIVERS DRIVING FOR 24 HOURS A DAY.

next two pages
FROM JULIACA THE ROAD FIRST CROSSES THE WIDE FIELDS OF THE ALTIPLANO (THE HIGHLANDS), BEFORE DESCENDING TO LA COSTA (THE COAST), THE THIRD CLIMATE ZONE OF PERU. THE COAST, WHICH CONSISTS LARGELY OF DESERT, IS CHARACTERIZED BY ITS CONSTANT MIST.

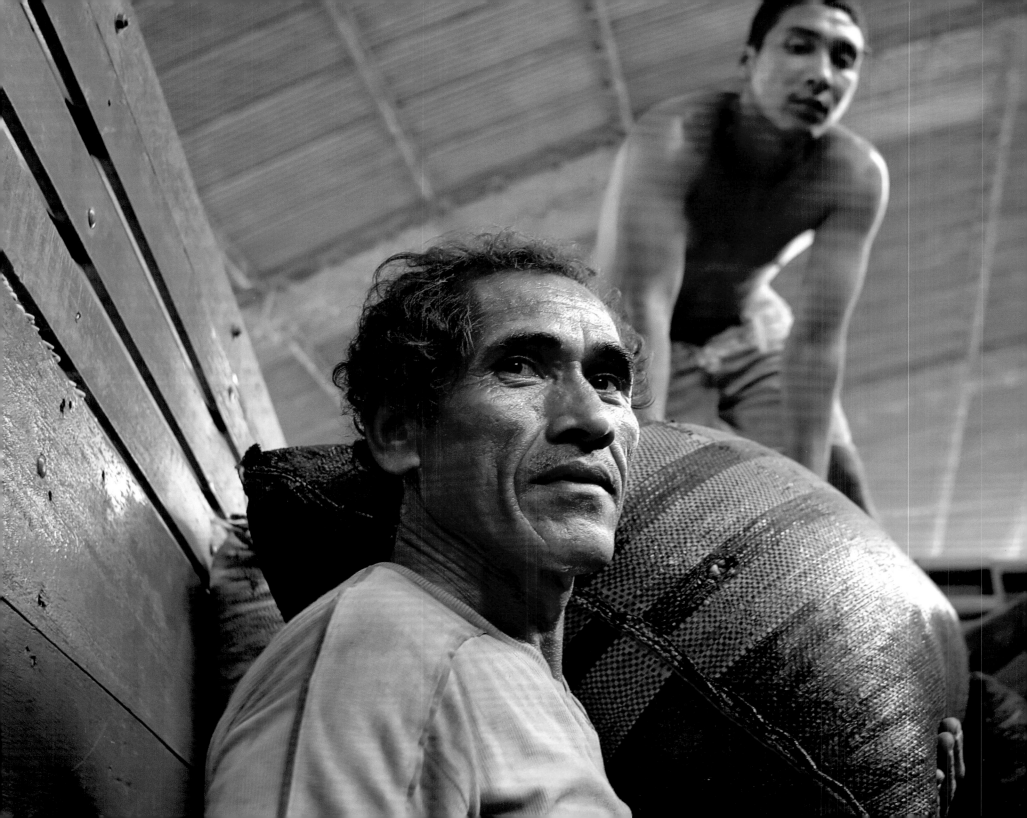

MIGUEL PAZ WAS BORN IN AN AGRICULTURAL FAMILY IN THE NORTH OF PERU. HE WORKED AS A TEACHER FROM 1992 TO 2001. IN 2002 HE STARTED TO WORK AS A SALES MANAGER FOR THE COOPERATIVE CECOVASA.

MIGUEL PAZ LÓPEZ: GLOBALIZATION AND ETHNIC NORMS 'THERE ARE MANY ISSUES IN MANAGING A LARGE COOPERATIVE LIKE CECOVASA. WE HAVE OVER 4500 MEMBERS CONSISTING OF DIFFERENT ETHNIC GROUPS – MAINLY QUECHUA AND AYAMARA INDIANS – ALL WITH DIFFERENT CULTURAL BACKGROUNDS. BESIDES FINDING THE BEST BUYERS FOR OUR COFFEE, IT IS MY TASK TO KEEP THESE GROUPS TOGETHER AND TO ENSURE THAT WE MAKE THE BEST COFFEE IN PERU.'

'I'm very proud to say that our cooperative has won the national cupping competition twice now. It is a direct result of encouraging farmers to work together, and giving them the right incentive to improve the quality of their beans. The winners even have a chance to travel to the USA, which is an immensely emotional experience for farmers that have never left their village. They are able to see their own coffee on grocery store shelves. It is a story that will be proudly shared for many years in the region, and it encourages other farmers to work on their skills and techniques.

'As a sales manager I always try to search for the best way to sell our product. Ideally, that means finding the highest price, so our farmers will get a chance to build a better life. However, this is not an easy task. Most of the problems in the coffee market are caused by fluctuations in production and price. Higher prices lead to more sowing, which in turn leads to increased production and decreasing prices. Afterwards, fields are neglected and a coffee shortage follows; as a consequence, prices rise again.

'On average, there is a worldwide overproduction of coffee so world-prices are low, often lower than the production costs. Small producers don't have the power to exercise influence over coffee prices on the New York Stock Exchange. Big coffee producers, coffee roasters and speculators have that power. So you need to be creative in your negotiations. There are millions of coffee producers in the world, most of whom live on or below the poverty line. To protect the social and economic interests of this group, many different certification organizations have been created to acknowledge that there isn't fair competition between big and small producers.

'Our cooperative works with different certifications, assuring us a better price, long term relationships and a healthier environment.

The beans are certified with the Fair Trade, Rainforest Alliance and Organic labels: all these certifications make it possible for us to invest in quality. By winning a national competition, we have also gained new opportunities to sell coffee in other markets – most importantly, specialty coffee markets. This is a new development which CECOVASA is following with great interest. But we have to be sure to keep our cooperative together. Without a cooperative, farmers are in a weaker position during negotiations and it is difficult for them to get export loans from foreign banks. As a cooperative we are able to get loans from funds like Triodos Sustainable Trade Fund and Progresso Fund which offer export loans at much lower interest rates and without the large demands of our national banking system.

'Within the cooperative we have to accept globalization – the reality of the world market – and at the same time preserve the values of native societies. The challenge is how to utilize the best from each culture within the cooperative. To accomplish this, we need two things: qualified management, and good training material that enables our farmers to educate their own people. This allows farmers to take on management positions and improve our operations. We want to be able to guarantee timely delivery of every order, and that is why everything from the production centre to shipment has to be coordinated perfectly. It's a difficult job.

'The single solution that solves everything in the coffee market is still far away. However, every year we see improvements. It is important that consumers understand the position of the coffee farmers in the chain. One day, we hope that you will come to Peru and see our beautiful plantations.'

THE BAGS ARE UNLOADED AT A FACTORY IN LIMA.

⬅ ➡

UNLOADING THE TRUCK IS PERFORMED IN THE SAME
WAY AS LOADING: BAG BY BAG.

FROM EVERY BAG A SAMPLE IS TAKEN. TECHNICIANS USE
THE SAMPLE TO MEASURE THE NUMBER OF DEFECTS AND
THE HUMIDITY OF THE BEANS.

← →

THE BEANS THAT ARRIVE IN LIMA ARE STILL PERGAMINO BEANS, WITH A THIN SKIN THAT MUST BE REMOVED BY A MACHINE. WHAT IS LEFT IS THE SO CALLED 'GREEN BEAN'. THE GREEN BEANS ARE PUT ON A ROLLING BELT. WOMEN PICK OUT THE DEFECTS TILL THE COFFEE HAS REACHED A CERTAIN LIMIT AS REGARDS THE AMOUNT OF DEFECTS.

THE WOMEN THAT PICK THE BEANS FROM THE ROLLING BELT OFTEN USE A SELF-MADE PLASTIC EXTENSION AROUND THEIR FINGER, TO MAKE THE PICKING EASIER.

BEFORE EXPORTING, THE SELLER AND/OR BUYER WILL
DO A CUPPING. EXPERTS WILL JUDGE THE AROMA,
FRAGRANCE, CONSISTENCY, AND TASTE PROFILES OF
THE BEANS. THE FINAL PRICE PAID OFTEN DEPENDS
ON THE RESULTS OF THESE CUPPINGS.

THE CONTAINER IS FILLED FOR A SPECIFIC CLIENT.
ONCE AGAIN THE BAGS ARE LOADED BY HAND,
BAG BY BAG.

A FULL LOADED CONTAINER CAN CONTAIN UP TO 400
BAGS OF COFFEE. AFTER FILLING, IT WILL LEAVE FOR
THE HARBOR. IN THE FOREGROUND ARE THE WORKERS
WHO PRINT THE LOGOS OF DIFFERENT CLIENTS ON
THE BAGS.

THE HARBOR OF PAITA IN THE NORTH OF PERU.
COFFEE IS SHIPPED FROM THE HARBORS OF
LIMA AND PAITA.

next two pages
THE JOURNEY OVER SEA TO THE USA OR EUROPE. THIS
WILL TAKE BETWEEN THREE TO FOUR WEEKS.

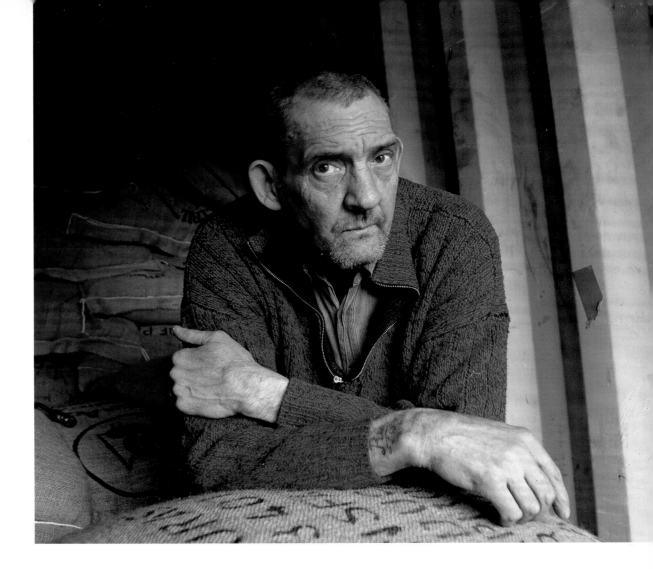

← →

AT THE DESTINATION THE CONTAINER IS OPENED AND
THE BAGS ARE UNLOADED.

next two pages
HERE WORKERS FILL UP A PALLET WHICH WILL BE
TRANSPORTED BY A FORKLIFT INTO THE WAREHOUSE.

99 →
14 ←

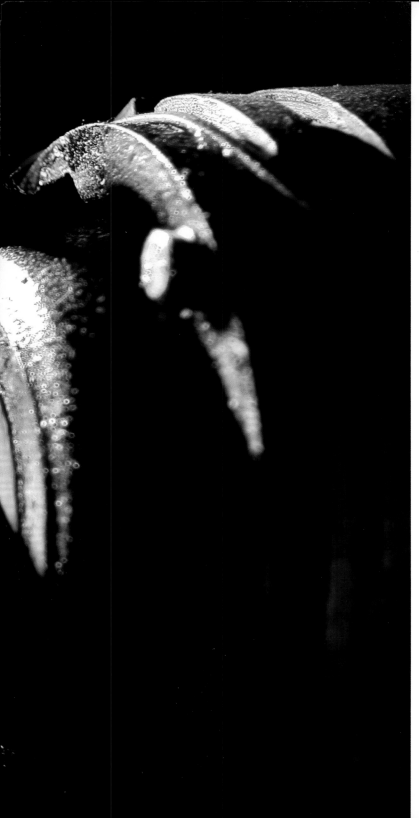

A ROASTER TAKES A SAMPLE OUT OF THE
ROASTING MACHINE DURING ROASTING AND SMELLS
THE AROMA. THE ROASTER HAS THE TASK OF
REVEALING ALL THE TASTES HIDDEN IN THE GREEN
BEAN. IT IS A DELICATE TASK, WHICH IF PERFORMED
BADLY CAN RUIN ALL THE EFFORTS OF THE FARMER.
TWO THINGS ARE IMPORTANT DURING ROASTING:
TEMPERATURE AND TIME. SOME BEANS ARE ROASTED
FOR A SHORT TIME AT HIGH TEMPERATURE, SOME
LONGER ON A LOWER TEMPERATURE. SOME ARE
ROASTED LIGHTER THEN OTHERS.

OFTEN, THE ROASTER WILL FIRST MAKE A SAMPLE-
ROAST TO FIND THE BEST WAY OF ROASTING THE
BEANS HE HAS BOUGHT. EVERY ORIGIN (EVEN
DIFFERENT REGIONS WITHIN A COUNTRY) CAN
REQUIRE A DIFFERENT ROAST – AND THE ROASTER
MUST ALSO TAKE INTO ACCOUNT THE TASTES OF HIS
CUSTOMERS. PEOPLE IN THE USA, FOR EXAMPLE, WILL
LIKE DIFFERENT KINDS OF ROASTS TO
THOSE IN EUROPE.

HEATHER PERRY: THE ART OF MAKING COFFEE

'PREPARING A GOOD COFFEE IS LIKE MAKING A WELL BALANCED MEAL. COFFEE CAN HAVE SO MANY FLAVORS WHICH ONLY BLOSSOM WHEN YOU REALLY PAY ATTENTION TO ALL THE DETAILS. I CONSIDER IT AN ART; SOME EVEN COMPARE IT WITH CREATING A SYMPHONY.'

'In a barista competition you need to make four espressos, four cappuccinos and four signature drinks in fifteen minutes. Timing is very important. In my preparation I will practice the whole thing over and over again, until I know exactly what to do down to the second.

'My preparations can take up to four months. First you need to decide which beans you want to use. Beans from Brazil have a different flavor character to beans from Ethiopia or Sumatra. So deciding which countries to mix is crucial. In my last championship I used Brazilian beans as a base because it gives a great body. The Brazilian beans also have very nice orange and citrus flavors, with great sweet chocolate undertones that were perfect for my cappuccino. I also added some Ethiopian beans to highlight the citrus flavors, but what this really did was add a berry finish to my espresso – a nice surprise when you are at the end of the espresso. To balance all the flavors I added some Sumatra beans. What I like about a good espresso are all those layers of flavors, waiting to be discovered while drinking it slowly to the bottom.

'I roast my beans separately. First I roast the Brazilian beans slightly dark and the Ethiopian lighter. Then I mix them and make the espresso, before seeing what needs to be changed. This process goes back and forth many times. With two different beans and three different roasts there are nine different combinations to try. With three different beans it gives you 27 possible combinations.

'Then you have to select in which proportion you are going to mix the beans. There are endless combinations, so finding the best blend with the best roast can take many weeks! After that, you have to decide how long you will leave the beans to rest before using them. I ended up opening the pack on the 8th day and using it on the 9th day. Then, if the settings of the grinder and the pressure of the machine are known in advance, you need to find out how much coffee you are going to use. Some coffees taste best when using 22 grams, others with 16 grams. I ended up using 21 grams of coffee and running it for 26 seconds through the filter. An important step in making a cappuccino is selecting the milk. The milk should not destroy the taste of the espresso – they should work together. The milk needs to foam in the right way and bring extra sweetness to the espresso. After the espressos and cappuccinos comes the signature drink – a drink you create using all your artistic talents. You can add all kind of extra flavors if you want, and present it in a way that suits the character of the drink. My espresso got a lot of citrus from the Brazilian and Ethiopian beans, and some terroir from the Sumatra beans I used. With the signature-drink it is about enhancing all these characteristics, and letting the flavors blossom in the best way by adding a few small extra ingredients.

My signature in the competition of 2007 was called *Espresso in the Clouds*.

Ingredients: Zest of a lemon, zest of an orange, 1 cinnamon stick, 1 vanilla bean, 1 tsp sugar, 1 tbsp Ginger.
Recipe: Combine all ingredients in a hot pan and top with 1 cup milk. Let simmer for 5 minutes. Take off heat to allow to cool for 3 minutes. Strain into whipped cream container and whip. Combine 1 egg yolk with 1 tbls brown sugar. Mix and top with 6 shots espresso while whipping with a hand whipper until foam begins to form. Assemble drink by squirting cream in the bottom of a tall glass and scoop espresso foam on top.

Enjoy!

THE COFFEE FROM PUTINA PUNCO, WHERE OUR
JOURNEY STARTED, IS FRESHLY POURED INTO A CUP.

 FARMER

Colophon

COPYRIGHT © 2008 OLAF HAMMELBURG, CONNECTING WORLDS PRODUCTIONS

PHOTOS AND TEXT (EXCEPT COLUMNS): OLAF HAMMELBURG
FIRST COLUMN: © KENNETH DAVIDS
SECOND COLUMN: © GEORGE HOWELL

DESIGN: TRAPPED IN SUBURBIA, THE HAGUE, THE NETHERLANDS
EDITOR: KIT BALLANTYNE, TWOFISH, AMSTERDAM, THE NETHERLANDS.
COLOR MANAGEMENT: RONALD MULDER, AMSTERDAM, THE NETHERLANDS
PRINTING: CHINALITHO
PRINTING GUIDE: HARRY KUIPERS, AMSTERDAM, THE NETHERLANDS.

ISBN 978-90-79531-01-1

ALL RIGHTS RESERVED. NO PART OF THIS BOOK MAY BE USED OR REPRODUCED IN ANY MANNER WHATSOEVER,
INCLUDING INTERNET USAGE, WITHOUT WRITTEN PERMISSION FROM CONNECTING WORLDS PRODUCTIONS, EXCEPT IN
THE CASE OF BRIEF QUOTATIONS EMBEDDED IN CRITICAL ARTICLES AND REVIEWS.

INTERESTING WEBSITES: WWW.TRANSFAIRUSA.ORG / WWW.MAKETRADEFAIR.COM / WWW.CUPOFEXCELLENCE.COM /
WWW.COFFEEREVIEW.COM / WWW.ROASTERSGUILD.ORG / WWW.SCAA.ORG / WWW.COFFEED.COM /
WWW.COFFEEGEEK.COM / WWW.COFFEERESEARCH.ORG / WWW.BARISTAMAGAZINE.COM

THE PHOTOS IN PERU ARE TAKEN ON COFFEE-FIELDS BELONGING TO THE FOLLOWING COOPERATIVES: CECOVASA,
COCLA, CEPICAFE, ORO VERDE AND PRONATUR IN PERU. THANKS TO ALL THE WORKERS OF THESE COOPERATIVES FOR
GUIDING ME THROUGH THEIR FIELDS AND MAKING THEIR CARS AVAILABLE FOR MY TRIPS.

THANKS TO: MY MOTHER JEANETTE TURKENBURG, HEATHER DEETH, CYNTHIA TORRES WONG, MARIEKE BRENTJENS,
TIENEKE BREEMHAAR, JOLEIN BAIDENMANN.

ALSO THANKS TO THE FOLLOWING COMPANIES FOR THEIR COOPERATION: INTELLIGENTSIA COFFEE, TERROIR COFFEE,
TRUE GROUNDS, SINTREX, ECT, NEGRISA (PERU).

SPECIAL THANKS TO: RODNEY NIKKELS (ORIGINAL BEANS), AND MIGUEL PAZ LOPEZ (CECOVASA).

SPECIAL THANKS TO THE SPONSORS:

Solidaridad

SOLIDARIDAD INVENTS NEW METHODS IN ORDER TO STIMULATE FAIR TRADE
AND SUSTAINABLE PRODUCTION. SOLIDARIDAD ALSO ASSISTS LARGE-SCALE
COMPANIES WITH TRANSFERRING TO CORPORATE SOCIAL RESPONSIBILITY
AND SUSTAINABLE PRODUCTION.
WWW.SOLIDARIDAD.NL

Triodos Ⓡ Foundation

TRIODOS SUSTAINABLE TRADE FUND OFFERS INNOVATIVE TRADE
FINANCE LOANS THAT ASSIST ORGANIC AND FAIR TRADE PRODUCERS IN
DEVELOPING COUNTRIES IN ACCESSING WORLD MARKETS.
WWW.TRIODOSFOUNDATION.NL
WWW.TRIODOS.COM/SUSTAINABLETRADE

TO ORDER THIS BOOK: WWW.CONNECTINGWORLDS.INFO / WWW.OLAFHAMMELBURG.NL

Connecting Worlds: The Coffee Trail

From consumer to farmer

Olaf Hammelburg

Connecting Worlds Productions